# Happiness Is Owning a Laundromat

## An Introduction to the Coin Laundry Industry

# Happiness Is Owning a Laundromat

## An Introduction to the Coin Laundry Industry

Sally Collins

Hopewell Publications

HAPPINESS IS OWNING A LAUNDROMAT: An Introduction to the Coin Laundry Industry Copyright © 2006 by Sally Collins.

Published by Hopewell
Publications, LLC
PO Box 11, Titusville, NJ
08560-0011 (609) 818-1049

**info@HopePubs.com**
**www.HopePubs.com**

Library of Congress Cataloging-in-Publication Data
Collins, Sally, 1932-
    Happiness is owning a laundromat : an introduction to the coin laundry industry / Sally Collins.
        p. cm.
    Includes index.
    ISBN 1-933435-06-2 (alk. paper)
    1. Laundry industry--United States. 2. Self-service laundries--United States. I. Title.
    HD9999.L383U632 2006
    338.4'7667130973--dc22

                                        2006013454

First Edition
Printed in the United States of America

*For the multitude of retired men,*
*divorced women, immigrants,*
*bus drivers, bartenders, doctors, brokers,*
*and any one else who has ever had*
*a dream of owning a small business.*

———————————

*I knew I was in*
*a highly desirable business*
*when my stockbroker left me*
*to open a coin laundry.*
*When my accountant expressed*
*a desire to go into business with me,*
*I just knew I had to write a book*
*about this wonderful, satisfying*
*career as a laundromat owner.*

# Table of Contents

# Table of Contents

# Table of Contents

iii

# CHAPTER 1

# AN EPIPHANY

You wake up in the morning and make yourself that first cup of coffee. You sit, your mind in a vacuum. The dreaded "R" word arises—"Retirement"—or maybe the dreaded "D" word—"Downsizing." What do you do? You have no hobbies, you'll have a lot of time on your hands, and you must supplement your income in order to survive. You recall what your father uttered with his last breath, "Get a cash business." Yes, but what sort of business? A franchise? A coffee shop? A hamburger joint? No way, not enough independence for you.

Later, as you pick up your dry cleaning, you notice a laundromat next to the dry cleaners. Hallelujah! Your mouth begins to water like Pavlov's dog at the promise of food. Why not? Everyone has dirty laundry, the investment should be modest, it doesn't look labor intensive, and all you have to do is collect the quarters. Right? Wrong!

Don't be discouraged. It's just a little more complicated, but isn't everything? There are rewards to owning a laundromat. You set your own schedule. You decide your own personal and vacation dates. And you work (or not) at your own pace. In other words, you are the master of your domain.

# CHAPTER 2

# OPTIONS CAN GIVE YOU DIBS

## THE OWNERSHIP OPTION

The first step to becoming super successful is to own the building that houses your most valuable and productive product—your coin laundry. More and more successful laundry owners are buying the real estate and either building a store or taking over the square footage in an existing building or strip mall. Imagine being free of landlords, leases, and asking permission to put up signs or do renovations to the façade of your building. Think of the calls you won't have to make about the leaking roof, and then having to wait, what seems like forever, for the repairs. You will be inclined to put more capital into your business when you know that you do not have a lease that is set to expire at a predetermined

7

date. You're the one in control of your business fate. More importantly, you can invest in new equipment (and save on utility costs, improve the look of your store and therefore can raise vend prices in good conscience), without worrying about how much time you have left on your lease to get a good return on your investment (ROI), in case you decide to sell your laundry at a later date. You can enlarge the store if your particular market requires it, or cut it in half and rent it out yourself if the economy dictates. You have the option to be a landlord. When you decide to sell either the business or the real estate, the main reasons for establishing a favorable sales price will be your net receipts and the option to give the prospective buyer a long lease.

There are a variety of ways to generate working capital, and banks love land, including the improvements on it. Use that property to establish credit with your bank, and you can make major improvements without filling out those pesky papers every time you need money. A line of credit is perfect for emergencies, such as a piece of equipment breaking down and in need of being replaced. You'll have the money immediately by writing a check provided by the bank when you opened your line of credit.

A term loan is best for long-term borrowing. This can be used for major investments such as installing central air-conditioning or a whole string of new equipment. Arrangements can be made to pay back the loan for a longer period of time, usually three to five years. Another source of loans is the Small Business Administration. They are receptive to small businesses because they get their money from a bank that receives a guarantee from the SBA that the loan will be repaid. Regardless of your choice, your real estate is your best collateral and the quickest way of getting cash.

The biggest advantage to owing the real estate is your option to sell your business, retaining control of the lease, and the ability to sell both your business and your property together. See what I mean about options? Take your pick! You can receive a monthly check, or a lump sum. What a way to retire! Without a doubt, owning property is the way to go and it contains your most valuable asset, your coin laundry.

## THE RENTAL OPTION

Having a landlord in a shopping center, a strip mall, or even a freestanding building is also an option. In that situation, your lease is your most valuable asset. The most common lease today is a triple net lease: rent, plus common area maintenance, plus taxes (your proportionate share based on your square footage). Triple net also includes your pro rata share of building insurance and may also include your share of property management. The ideal lease would be for twenty years, or ten years with two five-year options. This will give you the time you need to pay back any money you may have borrowed and be free of your mortgage debt for the remaining time. But what if you have a landlord offering you only five years on a lease? Unless you have some extenuating circumstances, walk away. The result could be equipment not being replaced. The operator, wisely so, does not want to make an investment based on the landlord's whim not to renew the lease. If you are financing your equipment, you know how the banks are—they want to know if you are going to be at that location for at least the life of the washers and dryers. Banks do not want to deal with used equipment in case of repossession. The problem for your creditor is that the repossessed value of used laundry equipment is extremely low. Using your laundromat as collateral means someone has to be a very good manager to retain its value and that's too big a risk for most banks.

Another factor to consider is a lease assignment, so that when you get ready to sell, you have the option to assign the lease to your buyer. If you are in a strip mall, you'll also want to negotiate an "exclusive" right to your particular service and ancillary services. You don't want another laundromat in your center, and you may decide to offer drop-off dry cleaning at some time, but you won't be able to if there is a dry cleaner in your center. Exclusive rights must be spelled out in your lease.

Of course, there is something to be said about renting. How about, "Mr. Landlord, the roof is leaking," or "Mr. Landlord, I need the snowplow over here." Get the picture? You rent the space. Mr. Landlord owns the problems. Be sure to negotiate a long-term lease that will exceed the amortization (time needed to recover debt) of the laundry's selling price. It must include a monthly rent with increases you can handle. This definitely keeps a good relationship with the landlord. It would be prudent of you to run any lease past a good real estate lawyer and your CPA before signing.

# CHAPTER 3

# SIZE MATTERS

## GET INTO THE MIX

OK, you found the perfect site for your laundry or you've negotiated a favorable lease; what's the next step? Deciding on equipment mix is one of your most crucial decisions. By that I mean the size and number of your washers and dryers. Two criteria will help you decide the right equipment mix for your market: location (city, suburban, rural) and demographics (singles, couples, professionals). This is when a demographic study of the site becomes invaluable. Demographics tell you population, age, income level, and family structure of your area. A demographic study can be obtained from your local Chamber of Commerce, the Coin Laundry Association or a local commercial real estate agent. It will also tell you the number of single and dual house-holds, immigration statistics, and the number of apartment renters. If you are in an urban location, your clients will most likely be in walking distance. If you are in a suburban location, study the demographics within a five-mile radius. A rural location could easily be a twenty-mile radius.

With this information, if your area is comprised mainly of singles or couples, you may decide you want mostly smaller machines (18 to 20 lb washers and 30 lb stack or single dryers) in your store. Stack dryers have just about replaced single dryers because they take up less space and thereby give you more revenue per square foot. Top load washers are also losing favor to the front load washers because of the energy saving features. If you're located near a university, you will find that students also prefer smaller machines. Of course, if you serve larger households with big families—a prime coin laundry customer—you will want to consider larger equipment (30, 50, or 80 lb washers and 75 lb dryers).

## WASH-DRY-FOLD

In a two-income household, a "wash-dry-fold" service, sometimes referred to as "fluff and fold," might be ideal for those customers who are starved for time. In a blue-collar area, or in any area where the husband and wife both work outside the home, time is more important than money. As a professional, you will learn that time is money. The customer drops off his/her dirty laundry in the morning, goes to work and finds all the newly washed and neatly folded and packaged laundry in the evening. In such cases, allow for extra machines for your attendant to use for this purpose. You'll also need extra storage space for the orders waiting to be processed, as well as a scale and a cash register. Incoming laundry is weighed on a scale, and the customer is charged by the pound, usually with a ten-pound minimum. Something to consider is a drive-through with a drop off window for wash-dry-fold services. If the banks and the fast food industry can do it, why can't you?

## YOUR BIGGEST COMPETITOR

Statistics show that approximately 7% of the population have used a coin laundry in the past 12 months. That leaves 93% of the population as potential customers, which means your biggest competition is the home washer and dryer (surprise, surprise), not another laundromat nearby. You may get these customers in once or twice a year to launder their king size blankets, comforters, drapes, rugs, or other large items. However, once they get used to larger machines—something they don't have at home—they may well become weekly customers. A homeowner with just one washer and dryer per household can wash five, ten or more loads of clothes at a coin laundry in the same time that it takes to wash one load at home by loading up five or ten washers at once at the local laundromat. When they have trouble with a leaky washer or a bum dryer, they just report it to the attendant on duty and the repairs are not their problem. Husbands really appreciate not having "repair washing machine" on their "honey do" list. Homeowners soon find that coin laundries give the best value for doing the weekly wash. Between repairs, cost of utilities and the original cost of the washer and dryer, it's far more economical to do the laundry at your corner coin-op. Today's coin laundry customers seek quality service, time savings, and convenience.

## STATISTICS THAT WON'T BORE YOU

There is not a number or statistic on earth as intriguing as discovering how many potential customers inhabit apartments with no laundry facilities. The magic word to look for in your demographic study is "apartment dwellers." If an apartment complex does have washing facilities, it's usually one or two pieces of equipment in each building, which means the tenant has to be lucky to find available machines. It could mean several trips back and forth, often up and down stairs, when only one trip to your coin-op would suffice.

Track the washing habits of this customer group, and you'll discover their preference of washer size. Most customers initially prefer the smaller machines with the least expensive vend price, but eventually gravitate to the larger ones, once they discover the convenience of loading all the family wash into one washer and the money they save. That's a win-win decision. For your benefit, the larger machines are more energy efficient, hence, lower utility bills, not to mention more revenue per square foot. For the customer, it's time and money saved. By contrast, the smaller machines are more price-sensitive and less energy efficient and take up just about the same square footage as the larger machines. You will still need the smaller washers for that occasional bachelor, senior citizen, or student with one load of clothes.

A distributor who sells washers and dryers is another source of knowledge. Look in the Yellow Pages under "Laundry Equipment." He can help in choosing the number and size of equipment, as he is the first to see the trends. Trust his judgment, and if you don't, find yourself another distributor.

Proper equipment mix boils down to maximizing revenue per square foot. Whether you serve a large family or couples/singles market, a suburban or urban location, larger equipment means greater income. Customers are the foundation of your business, but the right customer is more important than the total volume. The way to get the right customer is by catering to his/her laundry needs.

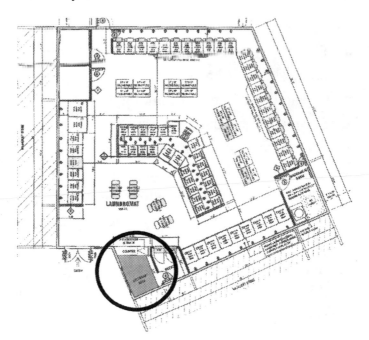

**Sample Blueprint:** Note the large "attendant area" for selling soap products and assorted laundry needs.

# CHAPTER 4

## GOOD TO GREAT

So, do you want to do just OK, or do you want to do great? The savvy operator will emerge with a larger than ever market share. What can you do to make sure that your coin laundry will be outstanding?

One way of expanding your customer base is by offering more services. Tanning beds, snack bars, video games, soap sold in bulk, laundry bags, or almost anything sold in your local dollar store can work. You must also become aggressive in your advertising, perhaps considering even television ads. Yes, it's expensive, but now is not the time to slash your advertising budget. Are you looking for a less expensive way of reaching your customers? Try direct mail. Be sure that your mailers feature color photos of your store, inside and out. If applicable, print your direct mail pieces in your customer's native language, as well as English, particularly if your demographic study shows a large immigration population in your area. Bilingual ads are sure to attract a broader base of potential customers.

Other advertising vehicles include radio and the Internet. The Internet is an especially effective medium in college towns as most every college student owns or has access to a computer. You can have a coupon for a free wash on your site that the student can print out, and bring to your store. Advertising in the Yellow Pages (don't forget to mention your wash-dry-fold service) is the old, but dependable means and cost effective way of promoting your store. What's more, don't forget to run promotions and drawings for free gifts. All are ideal for recognizing and rewarding repeat customers. A broad customer base and advertising will help you weather an economic downturn or conditions that will have an adverse effect on your laundry, such as a volatile stock market or a prolonged recession.

## CONTROL YOUR COSTS

Take a good, hard look at your variable costs. Is your equipment as energy efficient as it could be? If you have old equipment that is not contributing to the bottom line, get rid of it. Newer washers and dryers will not only save you money on your utilities bills, but they will justify a price increase. They will also give your coin-op a brand new look that will attract new customers. How the customer perceives your business is vital. That perception is the reality by which your business will be known.

## REVIEW YOUR FINANCES

Look over any mortgages or other long-term financial obligations that you might have and speak to your banker. Now may be the time to refinance. Read the newspapers and check the interest rates with competing banks. While reducing expenses, always maintain a high standard of service to your customers. A high quality of excellence, keeping up with repairs and maintenance, along with a fresh coat of paint, can separate you from your competitors. Now is a good time to plan, seek advice, and line up future creditors. Raise capital before you need the money. Take action early in a recessionary period, and you'll be ready for the growth that historically follows a downturn.

## FOCUS ON YOUR EMPLOYEES

Train them, put a uniform on them, and create an atmosphere of professionalism. "Career apparel" worn by your attendants provides instant recognition, improves employee morale by creating a team atmosphere, and it reflects/instills professionalism in the eyes of your customers. Give them opportunities to make decisions or, at least, to offer suggestions. Keep them informed. As an owner, you may have a vision of the future of your laundromat, but unless you share that vision with your employees, it's not possible to get them to work toward that vision. Be sure to spell out exactly where your business is going and how you hope to get there. Never forget; your employees are the key to your success. They represent you, the owner.

After instructing employees on what you need done, keep from meddling while they do it. Budget your time in another productive area. After all, working "in" your store means you have created a job for yourself, but working "at" your business means you have a career as an entrepreneur*.

---

* *Webster's Dictionary* defines an entrepreneur as one who organizes a business undertaking, assuming the risk for the sake of the profit.

## MENTAL SURVEY

Everything from your store's appearance, to the way your employees dress, to being involved in local activities contributes to how your customers view your coin laundry business. Be sure to donate time and money to local causes such as church festivals, the Main Street block party, or the high school yearbook. Offer to man a booth at one of the local organization's charity affairs, donate food to the town's Christmas effort to feed the poor, host a high school student as a future business leader, sponsor a local baseball team—in other words, be a good neighbor. Keep your name prominent by advertising in souvenir programs, local newspapers, and the local Chamber of Commerce's "welcome to the neighborhood" handout. A broad customer base, controlling costs, good community relations, and aggressive advertising will help you achieve your goals for your coin laundry. Who knows, you may own two, three, or four more laundries one day. Fess up, you've been thinking about it.

# CHAPTER 5

# COMPETITION IS GOOD

Perhaps your coin laundry is doing great, but the competition in your market is getting tougher. Even with revenue going up, the increased competition can shrink your profit margin. The opportunities are there. Make decisions that will satisfy existing customers and attract new ones. Think of a customer who spends $1.50 or so on a wash as putting a down payment on the $500 or more that he will pay you for over a period of a year. Multiply that $500 expected income by two, three, or four hundred customers a year. It adds up! You need to make sure that your clientele will continue to patronize your store. The average customer ranks doing the wash right up there with going to the dentist and stopping for gas. What's an owner to do?

## REVALUATE

You need an objective pair of eyes to look over your store and assess its strengths and flaws. When you see your business through your own eyes over the years, you tend to lose perspective. A new person—perhaps a customer, an attendant, or even your distributor—can use an impartial eye to notice missing tiles, burnt out bulbs, rust spots, walls that need a new coat of paint, and other unsightly messes too numerous to mention. They can tell you which areas need change or updating. Consider passing out a printed survey to your customers, asking them for their feedback. Today's customers are more discriminating than in the past. They are used to shopping in large chain stores (Target, Wal-Mart, Kmart, etc,) that hire professional planners—and that invites comparisons to your store. For starters, it's amazing what a gallon of paint and a general overall cleaning can do.

## LIGHTING

How about going a step further? A well-lit store gives your customers a sense of security and a high opinion of your business. Some utilities companies have created rebate programs to purchase energy saving products. Check with your local utility for the existence of such a program in your area.

But don't let the lack of a rebate stop you. Look for electronic ballast and econowatt bulbs, which last 30% longer than regular bulbs. There is a one-time cost for re-ballasting and re-lamping all fixtures. The cost depends on the number of fixtures in your store, but the rewards are many. Imagine your peace of mind if you never have to get out that ladder to replace a ballast, if your fluorescent tubes had a longer life, or if you no longer had visits from the local fire department due to a smoking ballast. At the very least, you will be pleasantly surprised when you get your electric bill! You will be lowering your air conditioning costs by using less heat per kilowatt, too. The tangible benefit is reduced electric costs, and the intangible benefit is reduced aggravation.

Don't forget to light up your parking lot for the highest security. If you have interior and exterior surveillance cameras, and you should, you need good light. Yes, this will increase your electric bill, but if you had it in mind to break into a store, would you choose the one all lit up or the one in total darkness?

Placing a mirror at any dark or blind spots in your coin-op is also a good deterrent for the bad guys. They never know when they are being observed. The employees and customers alike are able to see what is going on all over the store.

## WORK FLOW

You can have the most beautiful store in the area, but if your aisles are jammed with customers, bags of laundry, carts and kids, it's not pleasant, and that will eventually drive away customers. This is where your distributor can come in. He is a wealth of experience in the coin laundry industry at your fingertips. He can help you lay out your store, place change machines or a debit card system in a secure and illuminated area, reconsider the equipment mix, and even provide decorating tips.

Wide aisles (6 to 7 feet), folding tables placed across from the dryers, automatic doors, and available soap supplies, and change machines or debit stations in a safe and secure position, all make for a contented customer. Folding tables placed near the dryers are practical and appreciated by customers with large loads of clothes in their arms. The idea is to make this flow as simple and quickly as possible. Automatic sliding doors are another touch that seems to be made for a laundromat. Almost every customer who enters your business has his or her arms full!

Plenty of parking, close to the entrance of your store, is essential to a successful laundry. Most people don't care to do a lot of walking, especially if they are carrying a load of laundry. Placing your big machines near the entrance will steer your customers to them. A good design will do just that. It's the first stop they will make to get rid of that load of laundry. Large equipment will give you the most revenue per square foot.

Make sure your windows are not blocked by large signs, video games, or anything that prevents customers, as well as the police, from seeing clearly into and out of the store. If anything is placed in front of or next to the windows, it should be your coin changer or debit station, which will be visible from the outside in case anyone is messing with it during closed hours. The customer wants to be able to see outside and be seen inside. This creates a feeling of security, a number one priority for customers and employees alike.

## CASHLESS SOCIETY

A debit card system is the new kid on the block in the world of laundromats. A customer puts an amount of money in a debit station or card vault. The machine will dispense a card with the amount of money they inserted. He or she then swipes the card in the washer or dryer, and the price of the wash or dry is automatically subtracted from the card. The obvious benefit is that you don't have to deal with all those quarters, which can become quite heavy as you empty the coin boxes. With the debit card, the operator can raise vend prices as little as a penny. He's not tied into raising prices by increments of a quarter. You'll also build customer loyalty, as the customer has no other choice but to return to your store to use the card. A card system allows you to mail or hand out a card with three or four dollars on it as an incentive. The benefit to the customer is to be able to budget their laundry money by putting a certain amount on the card at the beginning of the month and not being able to spend it anywhere else. And they don't have to deal with those cumbersome quarters, either.

Competition is good. It keeps us on our toes, and we couldn't be as good without it. It's a law of economics that competition is the necessary catalyst for progress. A good floor design, the right equipment mix, an attractive décor, lots of glass, and a well-lit store will keep your business expanding.

The sweetest words are when a customer says, "I passed three other coin laundries just to come to yours."

# A Laundromat Makeover

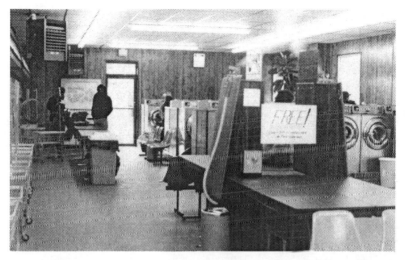

**Before:** a dull paneled room with no ambience.

**After:** clean vinyl walls and a bright, cheery atmosphere that doubled weekly sales.

# CHAPTER 6

# EARLY TO BED, EARLY TO RISE, WORK LIKE HELL, AND ADVERTISE

## ARE YOU WINKING IN THE DARK?

If you don't advertise, it's like a man winking at a girl in the dark. He knows he's doing it, but she has no clue. It hasn't been communicated to her. If you don't advertise, or communicate with prospective customers, no one knows what you have to offer, what a beautiful and efficient laundromat you have, or for that matter, that you even exist.

This can be easily remedied by taking the following steps to attract new customers, and keep the old ones; for one is silver and the other is gold. It's a fact of business life that it costs more to attract new customers, so it's prudent to keep the ones you already have happy and satisfied.

## TARGET YOUR CUSTOMER

Do you know you can go right into a prospective customer's home via direct mail? Advertise an incentive for coming into your store—not just a "free wash," but a generous offer of four free washes (perhaps worth $12), which is sure to get their attention.

There is a cost for you to have these flyers printed and mailed or delivered to cars and homes, so make sure the offer is worthwhile to the person receiving it, but it's not your only option. If you have computerized machines or accept debit cards, adjust the vend price to half-off on a certain day for one month. This will attract bargain hunters. Offer a special discounted wash and you might attract the senior citizens or those on a limited income. If you have the card system, try sending a card in the mail with several dollars on it redeemable in your store. You have nothing to lose if the card is not returned. Target every market you can think of. Remember you have the key to the coin boxes, so whatever coins that the attendant is putting into the boxes to start the machines when the customer hands her a coupon, will go right back to you. Your cost is the price of the utilities. And don't forget that clothes that come out of your washing machines have to be dried. That means an increase in your dryer revenue.

In addition, customers and their companions will get thirsty for a cold drink from your vending machine. Perhaps they need soap from your soap machine. They may buy a laundry bag from one of your attendants. Before you know it, your advertising is not costing you money—it's making you money!

## DEVELOP A HABIT

By offering four free washes or half-price washes once a week for a month, you will break a customer's habit of visiting another laundry, while establishing a new habit of patronizing yours. You've created a fresh routine for you and your customers.

If you advertise on a regular basis, such as four times a year, customers will look for your ads and respond to them. Consistency creates a routine, and this will add to your bottom line through an increase in gross receipts. You can be sure that satisfied customers will spread the word about your wonderful laundry facility, called "word of mouth," and it doesn't cost a cent.

## PLEASANT AMBIANCE

This is where we give back something in return for business received. It's not the free wash, which is advertising, but that which cannot be easily defined. It keeps the customers returning. It could be the way a laundromat looks and even the way it sounds and smells.

I'd like to offer you this perfect scenario: You're out to do the dreaded laundry. You pull up into a large parking lot and find a space right in front of the door. You gather up the kids, the laundry, and the supplies, and with your hands full, you walk effortlessly through the magic sliding doors into an efficient and well-managed laundry. Satellite radio (no commercials, no interference) plays softly in the background, as a helpful attendant greets you.

After putting your wash into the shining big machine and settling the little ones in front of a convenient TV, you sit down with a free cup of coffee. You relax. You're aware of a sweet, clean smell of baby powder, courtesy of an air deodorizer. On top of all this bliss, you notice a drawing for $25.00 worth of free wash. You fill out a paper with your name and address, and you notice last month's lucky winner on the bulletin board. You have a sense of anticipation at winning this drawing and a feeling of good will that no amount of money can buy.

Now compare this to a customer who pulls into your parking lot and cannot find a space to park or finds one that requires a long walk with laundry, kids, and soap supplies. As she holds the door open with a hip, she notices the attendant on the phone, several bulbs burned out, and out-of-order cards hanging from what seems like half the washers.

Which scenario would you prefer?

## PROMOTION PANACEA

Promotions are a way to keep your current customers happy and impress new ones. A favorite of both the operator and the client is a drawing for $25 or $50 worth of free washes. The cost of this drawing is negligible in relation to the benefits it can provide your laundry business. It rewards customers for their patronage, while also attracting new clientele. Even more, these drawings help build a mailing list that targets future mailings and other promotional efforts. And that's what it's all about —getting your share of the marketplace.

Other drawing prizes can be key chains, refrigerator magnets, calendars, or measuring cups with your laundry's name printed on them (all of which will keep your business name before the public). When you have to boost your vend prices, these little gifts make the increases a bit more palatable to the customer. It softens the effect. Think of advertising as a synonym for incentive. Incentive is what makes a person go past another laundry on the way to yours. So what are you waiting for? Stop winking in the dark. Spread the word about the best kept secret in town—your beautiful laundromat!

---

# CENTER LAUNDROMAT SAVINGS

| | |
|---|---|
| **Free $3.00 Wash**<br>**Center Laundromat**<br>1 coupon per visit<br>expires 1/7/07 | **Free $3.00 Wash**<br>**Center Laundromat**<br>1 coupon per visit<br>expires 1/14/07 |
| **Free $3.00 Wash**<br>**Center Laundromat**<br>1 coupon per visit<br>expires 1/21/07 | **Free $3.00 Wash**<br>**Center Laundromat**<br>1 coupon per visit<br>expires 1/31/07 |

# CHAPTER 7

# EVERY DAY IS LABOR DAY

Finding quality employees is one thing. Keeping them is another. Many employers are enhancing their benefit packages with non-financial, as well as monetary perks, aimed at creating a more relaxed and pleasant working environment. As companies grapple with how to attract and retain the best employees during a tight labor market, they could learn a few things about why employees leave and why they stay. In other words, it's not just about money. Good relationships with the boss, fellow employees, and customers, as well as support for their needs, are also huge reasons an employee will give for staying on the job.

## FLEX TIME

Flexible hours are especially important in giving employees some control over when and how they do their job. Varied hours and part time schedules recognize that people have different pressures at various stages in life. When a child is sick at home or aged parents need attention, both men and women need flexible hours. Being rigid about work schedules is a sure way to lose good workers, but helping employees to maintain a balance in their lives, makes them more productive and loyal. It also has a positive effect on the morale of the other workers when they see you have an interest in their needs. This means vacation time and personal days, too. Be up front at the time of their employment. Set the rules and rewards in the form of a job description.

## TRAIN 'EM AND DRESS 'EM

Employees who are well trained are much happier in their jobs, and a happy attendant is what we want. They know what is expected of them, as well as your store's policy regarding refunds. They understand how to handle clothing damaged by equipment and deal with an unruly customer. An attendant can look out for vandalism, theft, and abuse of your equipment and store. In other words, they are the eyes and ears of the owner/operator.

Occasionally we can forget our manners. Remind your staff that "good morning," "good afternoon," and "thank you," as well as how to properly answer a telephone, encourages a professional, friendly attitude among your staff and the customers. If you have a wash-dry-fold service, attendants will need training for the procedures that you want followed. Some operators give their attendant a share of the proceeds of the wash-dry-fold business. Just be careful that the attendant doesn't get so involved in getting that share, that he/she neglects the other duties of working in your laundry.

Uniforms are another idea that you will want to strongly consider. Coin laundry attendants are among the lowest paid workers, yet their clothing is subjected to more wear and tear than other similarly paid workers. Duties such as cleaning and polishing washers, cleaning lint from dryers, mopping floors, and taking out the garbage expose clothing to bleach and soap stains. A laundry by its very nature suggests clean, immaculate clothing. Even more, coin laundry owners draw from the same employment pool as fast food outlets, gas stations, drug stores, and grocery stores—all of which offer uniforms to their employees. Supplying clothing, or even providing a clothing allowance, is a perk that can help put laundry owners in a more favorable position to compete for quality workers. The highly recognizable look of a uniform sets an attendant apart in a crowded laundromat and instantly identifies him or her as a figure of authority.

## HOME SWEET HOME

A workplace that is free of physical hazards and the threat of harassment is a safe and secure dwelling. Make it into a second home for your employees. Include them in your decision making, set goals, assess how they are doing by meeting with them periodically, and provide regular feedback on their job performance. Assign chores to employees and then stay out of their way. Do not micromanage. Always reward workers for a job well done, although not necessarily with money. In fact, recognition and a simple "thank you" often work wonders. Give rewards for good work, accentuate the positive, and employees will feel connected to your coin-op's success. Don't forget birthdays, either. You know how good you feel when someone remembers your birthday. Everyone looks forward to a bonus at Christmas time, too. Don't disappoint. When you need a new employee, your first, and often best referral, will come from your happy worker. When employees refer their friends or relatives, it means that they feel good enough about you and your store to recommend the most competent people. Be sure to offer a bonus when someone makes a referral, providing that person is hired and stays for at least 90 days.

The bottom line is that replacing an employee will cost you money. The Department of Labor estimates that replacement costs are approximately half the salary of the person being replaced. Yikes! In addition, each turnover can prove to be a drag on the morale and productivity of your remaining employees.

We have a very fluid work force today, so it behooves all coin laundry owners to consider employee perks and bonuses - both tangible and intangible. Make your employee feel useful, valuable, and respected, and you might gain a long-term employee.

When your attendant leaves work after a particular trying day, you'll hope that he/she will think, "I'd quit today, but where else will I get all these bennies working in a laundromat?"

# CHAPTER 8

# GET-R-DONE

If you had a chance to build the ultimate self-service laundry, what would be on your wish list? First, you need a master plan. Consult a contractor with references and follow through and check out those references. Ask questions. When you get the answers and find them to your satisfaction, follow your gut feelings about the contractor. You didn't get this far in life without following your instincts. Your next job is to check with the town in which you plan to build your perfect beast. You'll want to know about zoning ordinances, setbacks, various fees, and impact fees. Impact fees are the fees charged in some states by the number of pieces of equipment you have and can be quite costly, sometimes prohibitive, to building a laundromat. The only way around this nasty problem is to buy an existing laundromat. You'll also want an architect, preferably one from the town you plan to build in, as he or she will know their way around the town's requirements. It also helps if they are familiar with the inspectors and engineers in that town.

## MAKE YOUR FOOTPRINT

Although it may sound backwards, first try to plan on what equipment will go into your fantasy coin laundry, as this will determine your square footage. A distributor will be extremely helpful at this stage, since he can sketch a preliminary drawing that you can take to an architect. Finished plans will be needed to obtain the proper permits. The distributor knows the sizes and other criteria of placing your equipment. Of course, he has a vested interest in helping you. When it comes time to purchase washers, dryers, coin changers, boilers, and even chairs and tables, he hopes to make the sale. In choosing equipment size and number, it would be wise to get feedback from potential customers. Consult demographics that will give you the ethnic make-up of your location, number of apartment dwellers, income, family size, and so on.

Don't forget the young, bored children. Especially when school is out, parents have no choice but to bring them along to do the laundry. You can round them up and herd them into an area as simple as a bench and a TV or as elaborate as a miniature playground. If you decide on the playground, check with your insurance agent regarding your liability. The least you can do is to provide some coloring books and a few children's games to occupy the little tykes. Parents will be grateful. Customers will bless you.

Video games are another consideration. They take up space, but also provide income. These can occupy your older customers, but of course, you'll need the square footage. You can buy the video games outright or you can make a deal with a company whose business is video equipment. The split of the gross is usually 50-50. If the game is out of order, you just make the call for repairs. Keep in mind you are in the laundromat business, not the video game business.

Plan on a small office for yourself or your manager. Add a restroom or two as required by your local ordinances, put in an attendant's booth, and you've completed your footprint.

## FOLLOW THE ROUTE

When a customer enters your store, his/her first thought is to put that load of laundry in a washer. Next, he/she will want soap powder, bleach, softener, and change to start the washer. You want to be able to move without bumping into other people. The coin changer or the debit card station in front of the attendant's booth can save some steps for the customer. There has to be a natural flow to this routine. Ideally, washers that are placed opposite dryers with folding tables in between, give you maximum efficiency. This will depend on the configuration of your space. Is it square, rectangular, or long and narrow? The most traditional stores are set up with an island of washers in the front and a bank of dryers in the rear of the facility. The large capacity washers are always up front, so the customers with heavy quilts and rugs do not have to carry them that far. As you can imagine, there's a great amount of flexibility to the layout of your store. Deciding what to put where can be challenging and fun.

Signage is another benefit to the customer. Make them positive and informative: the price of a wash, the time a dryer will run, the hours the store is open, please, thank you, welcome. These are positive signs. Signs with don't do this and that, and no to this and that are negative. Consider posting the signs in Spanish or any other language that represents the majority of your customers. This is a friendly, considerate gesture, greatly appreciated by newcomers.

## THE COMMAND POST

We also want employees to be comfortable and accessible. Your attendant's booth should be in the middle of the store, preferably raised by one step and visible to all customers. Conversely, the attendant has a full view of the entire store. Interior and exterior cameras placed in and around the store will be reflected on a monitor in the booth. This will show all the areas of the laundry and even the parking lot and entrances. This gives everyone, employees and customers alike, a feeling of security. This is a very important intangible, not to be underestimated in your ideal store. It would also be nice, and your customers would be grateful and loyal, to have an attendant that speaks their language.

The final step would be to turn your layout over to an interior designer for finishes and color coordination. Themed laundries offer something different. Maybe it's an elaborate mural with an underseas theme, or a 50's theme, or how about a 70's theme (think disco), or just a nice bright color scheme. It's going that extra mile that sets you apart from your competition. There is a certain expectation on your customer's part to observe and compare your store with the other businesses they frequent.

Now that you have all your ducks in a row—"Get-r-Done."

# CHAPTER 9

# ALL IN THE FAMILY

The same economic facts of life that apply to running your own business, also applies to couples and families running their own businesses. They take risks, succeed, fail, bounce back, and generally enjoy life together. Spouses, sons, and daughters can learn how to strike a balance between the challenges that come up every day in operating a small business and the rewards—real and imagined—that come from the dedication of meeting these challenges. The monetary rewards are obvious, but the interaction required of managing a business together creates a lifetime bond with family.

## MOM AND POP BUSINESSES

Couples who have left the corporate world to go into business together are back and in big numbers! He does the repairs and other manly chores, and she does the bookkeeping—that's the typical arrangement. Running a business is stressful enough, but being married to your partner is a move fraught with peril. There will be no more regular paychecks and no hospitalization or disability benefits paid for by an employer, however owning a laundromat can be a marriage made in heaven. Hiring siblings, cousins, and other family members can build strong family ties, as well as build a strong, flourishing laundry business. Naturally, for a business to grow, you'll need employees other than family members. Key employees will be the crucial factor to your success, and these will be selected according to the contribution that they can make to the business. If you have the type of employee who is comfortable approaching and interacting with customers, utilize this person's skills. He or she is ideal for the laundry setting.

By having regular meetings with family and non-family members, each one can express their concerns and perhaps vent a little. Develop a job description that lists duties and salary based on these duties. Give bonuses and awards in line with a person's talents and performance, not by their relationship to the boss. Give holidays off with pay and paid vacations based on their length of service. Develop a mission statement with the inclusion of all employees, and update it every year as dynamics change.

## SPECIALIZE

Dividing responsibilities with a person you know and trust is one of the benefits of a family-owned business. We each have our own specialties. One person is a people person, who should be visible helping and schmoozing with customers. The one that excels with figures can be put in the office to handle record keeping. Another may be mechanically inclined and enjoys working alone. This person is worth his weight in gold in a laundry. Perhaps a degree in marketing or business held by a relative can be used to push you in the right direction. Do not automatically follow traditional roles. SHE may exceed at making decisions regarding business strategies, while HE may be a great secretary. Let your talents dictate your responsibilities. Each person's strengths give you more confidence to manage a strong, successful business.

## TIME OUT

Getting away from your self-service laundry occasionally offers you a new perspective towards your business, even if it's only one day a week. All work and no play makes for a dull and unimaginative outlook on life, and your business will reflect that same outlook. Go for a drive in the country, visit friends, go fishing, do something that's fun. Personal time is important for your relationship, too. Nobody likes a workaholic. Some laundry owners are able to put their businesses behind them when they leave the workplace. Some incorporate their businesses into their lives. Regardless, you can't go home and complain about the boss. Whatever your personality and business strategy dictates, you choose the lifestyle you want.

No relationship will succeed without communication. Setting aside some time doing something pleasant, like lunching together, puts you in a positive state of mind and lets your mind open to discussions about employee problems, necessary building or major machinery repairs, and even evaluating the future of your laundromat. These discussions set the tone for the day. Outdoor or holiday family gatherings result in a relaxed mood that could be a good opportunity to resolve personal conflicts which may have arisen. Always make communication central to your business by running a business of inclusion. Inform employees about schedules, deliveries, and future plans. An uninformed employee will fill his/her head with the worse possible scenario. Encourage feedback and, just as important, criticism. A dissent does not mean disloyalty.

Finally, acknowledge that without your partner's help, you would not be where you are today. Have respect for one another. You have to be able to trust that your spouse or other family members are working to the best of their ability. Encourage them, even if they make mistakes, then forgive and forget.

## PASSING THE TORCH

It's not the most pleasant subject, but at some time, you'll have to talk about stepping down and naming a replacement. You can start preparing that person to step into your shoes when the time comes. If you foresee any problems with naming a successor, talk about it now and get everyone involved. Don't pick the person because he's your son or brother. Pick the person that can carry on what you've built.

The rewards of a job well done should be communicated to all employees. The benefits flow down to the customers, suppliers, and even the community. The end result of this partnership is a happy life and a growing, thriving laundromat business. And that's a good thing!

Sally Collins (Pres. NJCLA) with husband (Joe) and daughter (Pam), holding Leadership Award.

# CHAPTER 10

# FOUR REASONS TO REINVEST IN YOUR LIVELIHOOD

Did you know that small business owners have a chance to invest capital in their business and save money? That is, they can invest in new equipment and save at tax time. Because you are the captain of your business destiny, you have the better chance of controlling the risk. Of course, you could invest in Wall Street or in real estate, but a much better and safer investment would be to purchase new equipment or make other capital improvements for your self-service laundry. The fourfold advantage is explained in the following sections.

## DISABILITY CREDIT

Although the Americans with Disability Act has existed since 1992, many storeowners have not taken advantage of this law. Its intent is to ensure that the disabled customers have the same access to your facilities as able-bodied customers. This suggests the installation of frontloading washers and stack dryers, which are accessible to the disabled. A laundry owner may then deduct a tax credit of up to $5,000. Yes, that is a credit, which means $5,000 off your tax return. So, if you've been looking for a reason to get rid of your old top loaders or replace your single dryers, be sure to capitalize on this opportunity. Before purchasing, consult with your accountant so that you're perfectly clear on the benefits for your particular situation.

## ENERGY SAVER

All of this new equipment that you're going to purchase has another blessing that will become obvious once you receive your utility bills. The price of utilities will continue to rise. If you haven't bought new equipment in the last 10 years or so, you are in for a pleasant surprise. Today's dryers have an 80,000 or less BTU input, not as high as the 100,000 or higher BTU input of the past, which results in a lower gas bill. What's more, most front load washers now use 30% to 40% less water than older top loaders. Even hot water heaters are now 90% or more efficient. That means 90% of the energy is going into heating your hot water. If you go into your cellar or the room in which you keep your hot water heater and that room or cellar is hot, that means you are heating your cellar or the room in which you keep your hot water heater. Think of the time and money you can save, as most of this equipment comes with a labor and parts guarantee for a number of years, hence a reduction in maintenance costs and repairs and a big reduction in worry and stress.

## LOOKIN' GOOD

New equipment will upgrade your laundry to a state-of-the-art facility. Old customers will appreciate it, and new customers will be attracted to it. A renovation, even a small one, is bound to increase the bottom line. Everybody loves new. It creates excitement, where one person tells another person, who tells another person, etc, etc.

When replacing your equipment, rethink the size. Have the demographics changed in your neighborhood? You may want to replace your top loaders with front loaders, which are more family friendly and in the same time and space, produce greater revenue. A move like this will send a message to your customers that you are taking their needs into consideration. And while you're at it, if you have customers waiting in line to use your machines (oh, joy), why not consider an expansion? Maybe you can take over the store next door, or build an addition. If you want to stay in the game, you'll have to update your equipment and reinvent your business to maintain your share of the market. If you don't, the competition down the street will.

## INCREASE VEND PRICE

If you've been wondering when to raise your vend price, there is no better time then after you have purchased new equipment or put some other means of value into your store. Money that you spent has a softening effect on your customers and will make the price increase more palatable. Who would object to a modest price increase in return for the latest bells and whistles at their neighborhood laundromat? The increase in vend price will outweigh the few budget minded customers who might leave you. Anyway, you don't want the volume (too much wear and tear on your equipment); you want the customer willing to pay your price for his/her perceived value of your services. Survey after survey shows that price is not the most important issue for people—regardless of their socio-economic status. Your new look, plus the dependability of your equipment, will attract customers who see value for a fair price. You will attract the right customer in an upgraded, state-of-the-art, fully computerized self-service laundry.

So, what are you waiting for? Check out the newest equipment, see your banker, and reinvest in a business that has been good to you and can only get better.

# CHAPTER 11

# BUSINESS PARTNERS

Your family and friends may be the most important people in your life, but in your business life, three of the most important people are your lawyer, your banker, and your Certified Public Accountant. These are three professionals that you will rely on, at one time or another, for legal, money, and business advice.

## YOUR LEGAL ADVISOR, COUNSELOR, AND DEFENDER

Once you find the self-service laundry of your dreams or the perfect location for your laundromat, you'll want to consult with your attorney. An attorney can negotiate your lease, reaching an acceptable price

58

and length of contract. He or she acts as a buffer between you and the seller or landlord. There's always a way out when you're pressed for a decision. "I'll have to consult with my attorney" is a good excuse. Your attorney can also help you decide whether it is in your best interests to set up your business as a sole proprietor or to form an LLC or a corporation. The value of your lawyer doesn't end with the signing of the lease or bill of sale. There will be times during the course of that lease or ownership when legal problems will arise, and you will need a representative to go to bat for you. It's comforting to know you can pick up the phone and speak to someone who knows the details of your business.

## THE BRIDGE TO OPPORTUNITY

Economics 101 tells us that the single biggest reason that any new small business fails is due to a lack of capital. If you haven't done so already, establish a relationship with a bank and at least one officer at that bank. Check out the newspapers and consult with your business peers as to the banks that are the most favorable to small businesses. Don't make the mistake of jumping to another bank just because it can offer you a slightly better interest rate on your loan, because in the long run, loyalty is what counts to your bank. Establish a line of credit, whether you need it immediately or not. It will be ready when the opportunity arises. And if you're doing business right, an opportunity will arise.

Update your financial situation each year by submitting your personal financial net worth statement and current filed federal tax returns to the bank of your choice. It cuts down on a lot of paperwork when you need capital. It gets you off to a running start.

Having a business plan will also cut down on the waiting time when you need a loan. A good business plan should contain as much information as possible but be clear and simple to understand. You might want to state your reasons for going into business. Describe exactly the purpose of the loan and present a cash flow statement that shows how you will be able to repay the loan. It doesn't hurt to add a little personal information on your future plans for operating your store. It gives the bank a feel to your character and business acumen. When the gross receipts start rolling in after your self-service laundry is established, you'll need a good accountant.

## BUSINESS QUARTERBACK

The accountant's input is important in reviewing the contract before purchasing and selling the business. The purchase price of a business is usually made up of several components: equipment, furniture, leasehold improvements, goodwill, and a non-compete agreement. How you allocate the components could have a significant tax effect. We all know that it's not what you make; it's what you keep. Ask your friends for references, and interview at least three Certified Public Accountants to determine which one is best suited to your interests and personality, as this will be a long term relationship. For your final decision, rely on your instincts.

You'll need to make an appointment with your accountant at least every three months to do your quarterly reports. These can be very intimidating to a non-professional. You might ask your CPA when he will be doing your year-end planning. If he says, "After the year is over," do not hire him. Then it's too late. The year-end planning should be done at least in October after September's work is completed. It would be helpful to have a six-month meeting to see where you've been and where you're going, so you can make adjustments to your plan or pricing strategy, as well as a nine-month meeting to assess your tax situation. At this time, you will also do the year-end planning. It's best to find out now if you need to pay more estimated taxes before the end of the year, so you're not in for any unpleasant surprises.

A good accountant can keep you in touch with the shifting conditions of the stock market, which could have an adverse effect on your business and your personal finances. He or she can recommend payroll services, estate planners, and keep you informed of the ever-changing federal forms and acts of congress. When it becomes time to sell your business, his/her record keeping and advice on how to negotiate the terms of your contract will go a long way in getting you a top price for your laundry. In short, he or she can give you all the tools of the trade that you need to manage a flourishing workplace.

To this mix, add a distributor that offers more than just equipment for sale. He is pivotal to your store. He's on your side and has hopes of you turning to him when its time to replace your equipment. He offers services such as equipment repair, parts sales, new equipment and financing from the manufacturer. You'll want his knowledge, experience, advice, and yes, a shoulder to lean on.

In other words, the distributor you pick must be a smart and sympathetic friend.

Communicate regularly and nurture these crucial business partners—your lawyer, your banker, and your accountant—and the rewards will come back to you in the form of a thriving, profitable livelihood.

# CHAPTER 12

## NETWORKING PAYS

Call it networking or call it connecting, they both mean the same thing—the informal sharing of information among individuals or groups linked by a common interest. Business people with common interests and common goals will attend meetings and workshops and get to know each other. They can share their particular experiences and problems in the day-to-day operation of their self-service laundries. They can meet with experts whose sole purpose is to offer you the tools for business success and prosperity. Perhaps you need some advice about hiring or training attendants, finding a good repairman, or simply need to commiserate with a kindred spirit. You may want to compare the brand of equipment you purchased with another operator's brand. Interacting with your peers can help you solve such problems, and it definitely will lessen the stress of being isolated in your own business. Sometimes you become so intent about going about your daily routine, that you forget there is a world out there.

## COIN LAUNDRY ASSOCIATION

There is no better place to start networking than by joining the Coin Laundry Association, a national organization, exclusively devoted to the laundromat owner. Check with the CLA, ask for an application, and sign up now.

The CLA offers several "members only" benefits. Their insurance plan is tailored to the laundry owner's specific needs. Workman's Compensation plans are also available. Are you interested in finding a location and building a new laundromat, marketing your current laundromat, or keeping your laundry safe? Do you need demographics? If you decide to sell, do you need a formula to set a realistic selling price on your valuable asset? Maybe you want more information to decide if you even want to be in the coin laundry business. All these questions and concerns can be answered at the various workshops that are held several times a year in different cities within the United States. Literature is also available and can be mailed to you. Visit this valuable and informative organization at www.coinlaundry.org.

The CLA's big meeting is the CLEAN Show (www.cleanshow.com), held every odd year in cities like Las Vegas, Orlando, and Dallas. Thousands of national and international members, nonmembers, manufacturers, distributors, single and multi-store entrepreneurs are welcomed to the world's largest textile care exposition. Attend one of the many educational sessions and you're sure to come away with the knowledge to implement your goals. A panel of experts will be on hand to offer tips and strategies for all phases of your business. After a long day of soaking up all of the latest products and innovations from around the world, it's off with the family and friends to all the attractions these wonderful cities have to offer.

And it's tax deductible! The business part of your trip, that is. Get and save receipts to isolate your business activities from personal days. Hand them over to your accountant to allocate the proper expenses that will earn tax deductions. Charging everything on a credit card is a good idea.

## Manufacturers

Over 500 exhibiting companies, spread over up to 225,000 square feet of exhibit space, will be in attendance at the typical CLEAN Show. Are repairs your concern? Having trouble with your coin changers or an old, inefficient boiler? Want to check out the latest in laundry carts, folding tables, or bill counters? How about laundry bags, uniforms or the latest in security equipment? See on-the-spot demonstrations of security systems that enable you to sit back in your lounge chair at home and observe your laundromat on your video screen or turn on your PC or laptop and remotely monitor the operation of your laundry from anywhere in the world. Watch what your attendants are doing or not doing, and see if the cleaning people are performing their job. If not, pick up the phone and surprise them!

In any case, you are guaranteed to go home with names of key contacts, along with a slew of important business cards and personal recommendations; that is, if you don't make your business deals right on the spot. Special pricing is offered at the show to CLEAN attendees. The CLEAN Show is a wealth of riches, not to be missed by all serious entrepreneurs.

## LOCAL HELP

If you are unable to come to the big cities for the CLEAN Show, have no fear, your local distributor has the same get-together, but on a smaller, more intimate scale. Distributors invite their customers, repair people, and prospective customers to a service school, usually held once a month. You will have a hands-on demonstration of the latest equipment by experienced repairmen and representatives of the various manufacturers in an informal atmosphere. While you're there, pick up your needed supplies in the parts department and visit with your local laundry owners to catch up on the latest happenings that directly concern your livelihood. Refreshments are usually served, making it an enjoyable and educational way to spend an evening.

There is a positive advantage to being a part of an organization. It's a catalyst that enables business people to accomplish collectively what no one can do individually. CLA has the technology to solve your problems. The technology is the combined experience and knowledge of all of the members combined.

Join the most informed, professional, and successful people in the self-service industry at these affairs and meetings along with those who provide services to the coin laundry industry. These people are the cream of the crop—dynamic and prosperous, creative and independent. Networking indeed pays! Are you a networker?

Sally Collins and John Vassiliades (Chairman of the CLA) man the CLEAN Show reception desk in Las Vegas, Nevada.

# CHAPTER 13

# PROFIT POTENTIAL

## HOW MUCH MONEY CAN I MAKE?

This is a valid question, and the short answer is approximately 30% of your gross. The long answer is far more complicated with loads of variables such as:

*Debt Service* – How much did you borrow to invest in your business and at what rate of interest? Check with other banks periodically for a lower rate.

*Rent* – Hopefully, you negotiated a favorable rent, but if not, don't be bashful about going back to your landlord if high rent becomes a problem. He'll be more likely to negotiate with you than lose a tenant.

*Payroll* – If you, your spouse, or partner plans to operate the store personally, you will lower the labor cost factor. Consider an unattended or partially attended store.

*Maintenance* – If you are planning to do your own repairs, you can lower your costs. Often when purchasing equipment, you will have a one to five year guarantee on parts and/or labor. Look for this deal.

*Utilities* – Aim for 19% to 26% of your gross to supply your gas, electric, and water. Solar heat can help you out here, if it's feasible. You might also consider a well if it is sanctioned in your area.

*Vend Price* – You'll want your vend price to be somewhat competitive, but as long as you are operating a good store, it's a wonder what a raise of a quarter on your washers can do to the bottom line. Your drying time can also be lowered slightly.

*Hours of Operation* – Open earlier and close later than the competition. Think about opening 24 hours, but first check with local ordinances.

*Insurances, Supplies, Miscellaneous* – These items should comprise 3 to 5% of your gross. Check with several insurance companies that deal exclusively with laundromats.

## PRO FORMA CASH FLOW PROJECTION

A distributor can make a projection of a new store's income and expenses with a Pro Forma Statement. These estimates are based on the income produced by the washers and dryers and any other ancillary services, such as Wash-Dry-Fold, soap and soda and candy vending machines. Treat these figures with caution. They do not guarantee profitability, since this is not a legal document. Here is an excerpt from a statement that was prepared for me:

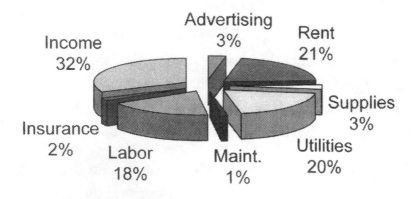

**Example Pro Forma Breakdown**
**Note:** Many factors, including geographic, economic, and demographic conditions, determine profitability.

# CHAPTER 14

# EXIT STRATEGY

## KNOW WHEN TO HOLD, KNOW WHEN TO FOLD

Eventually there comes a time when your business will change hands. If you were smart, you would have started making your plans long before this time arrives, but have no fear; it's never too late. Perhaps you've been mentoring a certain person, one that you've trained and prepared to take over the reins, or maybe you plan on selling your business, taking the money, and moving to a state that has a more agreeable climate and tax situation than the state you live in now. Maybe your son, daughter, or other family member is qualified to follow in your footsteps and keep your business perpetual. Not to worry. Regardless of which criteria you choose, you still have time for a master plan.

## THE NEXT GENERATION

For openers, why not have a family powwow? When you're planning on passing your company to a family member, you'll want them to know your intentions. Bring this up for discussion and find out who is interested in a life as a laundromat owner and who has other goals in life. In order to have an orderly transition, you must first choose a successor and give him/her the authority, education, and any other necessary tools to carry on in your place. You may want to hang around for a period after the succession to ease the new person and the customers into the new ownership. Your successor may have grown up in a business climate different than yours and, thus, have different ideas about making decisions and taking risks. Listen to him/her and evaluate whether you want your business to go in that direction.

Now for the crucial decision: How do you arrive at a sales price for your laundry?

## THE MULTIPLIER METHOD

Laundries tend to have a similar pricing formula as other small businesses. They use the multiplier or rule of thumb method: multiply 2 to 5 times the business's annual net income or 1 to 2 times the annual gross receipts. A laundromat has the edge over other small businesses because it has a cash flow, provided it has been managed properly. Buyers today are interested in the net profit, commonly referred to as "the bottom line." The multiple factor depends mainly on the age of the machinery, the length of the lease, the location of the business and the competition.

Take a look at some examples using the annual net income method: If the general condition of the store is poor, has bad lighting, a short lease (less than five years), is in a high crime area, and has equipment more than ten years old, the multiplier is two times the annual net income.

If the general condition of the store is good, has a lease for 10 years or more, and has a good location but needs a little work, multiply the annual net income by 3 to 3.5.

A real winner has an excellent location, plenty of parking, air conditioning, a long lease (10 to 20 years), newer equipment (2 to 4 years old), and a modern overall condition. Multiply the annual net income by 4 or even 5 and, congratulations, you've made a great deal!

## CAVEAT EMPTOR

The multiplier method is not a formula carved in stone. Although it is the most common and simple method, there are so many more facts to take into consideration. Competition is one. If the competitor's store down the street is small (1000 to 1500 square feet), dirty and filled with old equipment, there's not too much worry there. If it's a 5,000 square foot store and expertly managed, the multiplier would have to go down. If the buyer plans on adding new employees, doing away with certain ancillary services, such as wash-dry-fold, his projected net income will go down. The buyer's desired net income will be different than the seller's present net income. Adjustments have to be made between the two parties, the accountants, and the broker.

## RETURN ON INVESTMENT (ROI)

The buyer who has money to invest is looking for the best return on his money. There are a lot of passive investments out there that can give you 6 to 10% without the hassle of running a business. If a seller shows a net profit of $50,000 a year and a buyer pays $500,000 for that business, the buyer is making a 10% profit. Most laundry and small business owners would like to make a 20 to 25% profit for their efforts. Adjustments have to be made on the part of the buyer and the seller. This is where negotiations come into play. Ultimately, the selling price is determined by the amount the buyer is willing to pay and the amount the seller will accept. One last factor is timing. When the economy is less prosperous, prospective buyers are less willing to pay.

## WORDS OF WISDOM

Owning a laundromat can be a satisfying, productive, and lucrative part of your life. Think of all the people you'll meet, the service you will provide, and all the while making a respectable living for you and your family. You can retire on your own timetable or keep on working past the usual retirement age. The choice is yours. A laundromat is one of the few businesses in which a customer pays cash in advance for his services— no bad checks, no credit cards, very little inventory, just a nice, steady cash flow. Because it is an essential service, laundries are known to be recession proof. Clean clothes are a necessity; there will always be an infinite supply of dirty laundry. Your father would be proud of your decision to own a laundromat!

When it's time to hand over the baton, recall the words of the Chinese philosopher, Lao Tsu, "Retire when the work is done. This is the way to heaven".

# INDEX

# ABOUT THE AUTHOR

**Sally Collins** and husband, Joe, own three successful, national award-winning coin laundries. She is a founding member and the first woman president of the New Jersey Coin Laundry Association (NJCLA), and as an elected board member to the national CLA, she served as its chairman. Ms. Collins publishes articles on coin laundry management, conducts workshops, and sits on local and national laundry panels. During a lifetime of breaking barriers for women, she acts as mentor and consultant to fellow laundry owners and prospective owners.

Printed in the United States
78421LV00002B/10-18

9 781933 435060